In That Moment...

Inspiring Words That Will Guide You

Lindsay Woods

Although the author and publisher have made every effort to ensure that the information in this book is correct at press time, the author and publisher do not assume and hereby disclaim any liability to any party for any loss, damage or disruption caused by errors or omissions, whether such errors or omissions result from negligence, accident or any other cause.

All rights reserved. No part of this book may be reproduced in any form or by any electronic or mechanical means, including information storage and retrieval systems, without written permission from the publisher or author, except in the case of a reviewer, who may quote brief passages embodied in critical articles or in a review.

Copyright © 2021 Lindsay Woods

All rights reserved.:

ISBN-13:

Table of Contents

1 12

2 13

3 14

4 15

5 16

6 18

7 19

8 20

9 21

10 22

11 23

12 24

13 25

14 26

15 27

15 28

17 29

18 30

19 31

20 32

21 33

22	34
23	35
24	36
25	37
26	38
27	39
28	40
29	42
30	44
31	45
32	46
33	47
34	48
35	50
36	51
37	52
38	54
39	55
40	57
41	58
42	60
43	61
44	62
45	64

46	66
47	68
48	69
49	70
50	71
51	72
52	73
53	74
54	76
55	77
56	78
57	80
58	82
About the Author	83

INTRODUCTION

The journey of writing this book has just been incredible. It never made any sense to me as to who I am or where I was in my life. I never realized I was starting a new journey. I just decided that I was tired of thinking and feeling the way that I thought about life. This book is written with a simple intention of just wanting to help. I was in such a terrible place in my life that I have never in my life thought I'd be in But I started not like some but more as most do.

I was sad and depressed. I didn't think very well about myself. You can name it all and I felt everything I should not. I thought I was the ugliest person. I did not think I was very funny, and I thought that I deserved all the ill that came to me, I would say I'd like to think that I might good person. I grew up in negativity, anger, hatred, and even blamed others for my failure. Because of the way that I thought that life, in general, was for me. I think upbringing also plays a role in how we see the worls, and there were some great things I picked too. There were many things that my Father and my grandparents taught , I didn't completely grasp until recently. As a kid, my grandpa would listen to audiotapes for an afternoon nap. So, when I was 9, I would listen to one of the tapes of Jose DeSilva: the DeSilva method.

Interestingly it helped me. But I was way too young to understand a lot of it then. A lot of what I learned didn't come along until 2019 when I joined this online marketing thing. That's when I learned how mindset changes your life. THIS WAS MY LIFE-CHANGING MOMENT. I left everything and decided that I was going to change everything about me and who I was. I couldn't understand more now than I did when I was 9. This was always there; I couldn't be happy unless I wanted to be. So, I became happy.

I started working on self, its still a long journey but even the tiny steps have brought in huge shifts. I feel like a new gate or doorway is opened through writing.

I have several things I am working on. I also realize that its not just me going through these changes, with me there are so many who are walking this path of changing self, looking at things differently, living a better and a fulfilled life, I am not the only one. I started writing on my Facebook Profile. . It all started to click together I was a good cheerleader. I was inspiring people as went on my journey. It became this beautiful essence of who I was and what I did for others. I should have reached my goal of 250,000 smackeroos by now. But that not what's in my heart. My heart ached I would get messages from people all over the world, including my community saying "I love your posts thanks you helped me get through a rough day." I learned I am inspiring people more than I thought. So, one day as inspiration hit me I decided I wanted to write my thoughts out and eventually it slowly became a book. Remember that we are completely human, and this is like a journey that's supposed to happy and fulfilling to us!

This book can be read one chapter at a time, or you can let your intuition guide you and open a random page and it would be the message universe wants to give you in that moment.

I believe that love is all we need in the end.......

I hope you find inspiration, hope and love through this book.

ACKNOWLEDGMENTS

In the beginning of this journey, I took so much with me from all who have been in my life; these people have been so patient with all I have gone through.

My first thank you is to the two most important people in my life:

My child Chennay (Ty), You were always my inspiration to be more and better than yesterday. I have all I could ever want with you as my kid. I will always say that you saved my life. You have been my shining star, made my days brighter. when I found out I was going have you I felt that what was always missing was on it way to me. I was given a true blessing to be able to be your Mom. The path that was laid out before me was much different than I thought at first! I love seeing you grow more everyday into the beautiful person you are and will become. Your kindness and love for all is astounding to me. The way you see the world gives me understanding that is foreign to me. I am always forced to see things and look at life so much differently. I love to see you smile, laugh and being happy. All we have faced together learning more together everyday is just amazing. You're my pride, my joy and my everything.

Toyin, you have always been a force to be reckoned with! You stand stronger than anyone I know. You helped me discover things about myself. You became more than a best friend, you became Family. I can't believe that so many years have passed, and we still can get so busy with life, but still a few months later call and chat like no time has passed. I am so happy to have your Undying support and belief in all I do! The love of a great sister comes in time, times I have always smiled. The I see in front is different from the one I met! But that means you have grown and become so much more. You believed in me when no one else did, I can't thank you enough for everything that you brought to my life. I have a hard time thinking about what to say as great thanks other than to smile and say, "I Love you." Your always there no matter you help make this book possible. Without you and all you have encouraged this book never would have come to be. "I got this one" is always the saying……… everyday you make me want to be better. Thank you for believing in me.

Snehal, your one my biggest inspiration and been my mentor all the way. You didn't hold my hand but gave the basic steppingstones to make this all a reality, I can't thank you enough for all you do for me. The love, appreciation and kindness are always there. You have helped so many. How can I thank you enough for everything that has come to me since meeting you? Its been amazing to know that I have such amazing supportive people in my life. Snehal, you have slowly become family and I love it! Our journey with this book has just begun. But I know that we will have many more to create together. My dream of being an author has become reality. And I have you to thank for that.

I have so many to thank in this journey and I can't say it all, so I am going to say it here! You all know who you are you're the ones that have made this dream livable. Supported me in ways that I can't even begin to explain the smallest things like you got this! And the I'll be all over the book when it launches, I am so excited for this!

All my friends and family have been the most gracious and undying support and love that I needed when I needed them the universe takes to all the people; we need in life including recently. All my life I have looked for the right friends. I have so much to be grateful for in this world. All whip has been there for throughout this have been my rocks, my cleaners (dishes the house in general) my kid and my other half have been the most amazing supports ever their love and encouragement have not been without acknowledgment.

We always save the best for the last. Scott, I am not sure how to thank you. I have yet to figure it out, you have done so much for me in this journey that it wouldn't be possible without you. I have the best friend one ever asks for and that's you and I could go on ands on an on and on but for I have to say simplest THANK YOU VERY MUCH.

Love

Lindsay

1

When you stop and see the world as it is
You open a new window
View the world with love, happiness, and smiles.
I can't believe we've made it this far.
Nothing better than making it.
When you reach the other side, it's like "Oh My damn"!
"How did I do this?"
Self-reflection is key, being honest with yourself is just the start
Can you say that I love you and I am grateful for you?

2

Can we do something today?
How is it that you and I are all the same and yet so different?
I need to say 'love' is why we are the same
Love is why I don't care that we don't always see eye to eye
But I know you have a heart of gold, so don't stop
Can you make someone else's day by being kind?
There's something about saying "hi" and smiling
Say to the gentleman "Good day Sir" with a smile
He might be needing that today.
If you feel bad about yourself, pay for someone's coffee
You might just make someone's day better.
Remember we are the essence of love

3

Learn to live every day with gratitude
Give love to everyone that you see
Make it the best day for somebody,
Show kindness to the person in the corner whom, no one bothers with
They could be in your office,
The elderly person down the street
We need to love, not hate.
If you feel negative; go for a walk around your neighborhood,
Look at all the houses and wish them love and happiness
See it'll make you forget about yourself and see the world.
Wish love, peace, and warmth to each home

4

Today find things you don't need and give it away
Even if it costs a pretty penny but never wear it.
There's a person who'd love it and would make use of it
Anything you have that is clutter to you is a treasure to someone else
Can you see someone loving like you did once?
I know I love doing this.
This helps me feel good about my day
It is best to be loved, where there's appreciation.
If you see it for sale, don't be mad.
You never know what that person faces,
They may need those 5 bucks.
Wish no ill will on anyone,
only wish them The Best

5

All I want is love for the world,
Do it every day with gratitude,
in every step you take,
I am going to be happy and filled with love today
As I love me and all I am today
I will not regret what I have done,
Some of it I'm not so proud of,
All my experiences have created the "me", I am today
I love me and, make it my goal to be love.
I can do anything I want if I have passion and love
Can there be a day where you allow yourself to be comfortable?
I say Nah, you should find things that make you uncomfortable
Because you grow, you will grow and be beautiful
I love the butterfly for this,
it has so many stages but from beginning to end.
it is a beautiful sight to see.
there is nothing more beautiful than growing.
You are aware of yourself and your true self.

How can you be comfortable and keep doing what you are doing?

Stop being comfortable and go try a new food that makes you uncomfortable.

6

I sit and watch,
I am watching myself,
I am aware of all that I do,
I realize that I am Love
I have been and always will be love,
I understand my path more than I did yesterday
I needed that pain to see what I needed to learn
I am Right where I need to be
I am free and I'm freer than ever

7

I wake up each day, look at me and realize
I need to smile more but I must just BE,
So, wake up to you and only you,
You're the one that must make you smile
Start your day with a smile and an I Love you,
Make it worth your while,
YOU ARE WORTHY OF YOU

8

Have you ever watched the sunrise?
Its something to check out,
The gratitude that comes with it.
The beauty that arises in the experience is astounding
Let that be your start to another beautiful day in our amazing world
Say to yourself like a friend of mine says to all
"GOOD RISING"
we all arise like the sun
so be the arising of the sun
to the new day before you
share that light with the world

9

Good rising to you,
We can be our own toxicity
Are you toxic?
Did you say 'no' to that?
Ask again, but be honest this time "Are you toxic"?
Bet you said 'no' again
I bet you're the most toxic to YOU!
I am toxic to myself and say bad things.
I am my toxic relationship with me,
I have to say nice, kind, loving things.
I can't, I won't, and I don't become non-existent
Say I CAN, I DO, AND I WILL
You will succeed faster when you love you

10

You are not the same as you were yesterday,
It is all about growing and learning about you,
Love, peace, and happiness will come
in a truth that is warmth for the soul
That warmth becomes your blanket of peacc,
When that blanket becomes too comfortable
Ask yourself "Do I need to get a new one for some change"?
Or are you at your one true self?
NEVER be comfortable, be satisfied but never comfortable!
Always work away from being negative and be more positive
Never allow yourself to be negative,
it'll make what bad you hear, easier on you
Listen to friends but, don't allow it to be your undoing
Negativity is always an undoing.

11

Allow your haters to hate,
Someone will always have an opinion,
Remember that you are all that matters
Your Opinion of you is all that matters
Say to yourself in the mirror
I am loving
I am strong
I am funny
I am beautiful
I have all that I need right now
I am happy
I am satisfied with who I am becoming
I am loving myself more every day
I am perfectly imperfect.

12

As I learn ME as I am
As I accept myself as I am
I will not allow my fear to control me and my every movement
I am all I need,
Everything that I am is enough for me
Who I am is also MORE than enough for those who love me as I am!
I know I am worthy of all things that will come to me
I deserve my happiness and what makes me happy,
There's a lot to me as I am human
I am a person who is complicated to most
But those who "get me" love me doing me
So, live you according to you
Not what others think of you!
I love you, as you are right now

13

Life is hard,
Life is complicated,
Where does one go to find happiness?
We find it all within us
We are humans and beautiful at that,
We bring light to the darkness within us
We also bring that darkness to ourselves,
That's why we say:
There is always a light at the end of the tunnel
Be your light in your darkness,
But also try being the light for others,
They may need a little extra love and light
Their light might be shining but it just barely,
So, help them walk that path and show them they can make it brighter.
So, they can help others light theirs brighter.

14

Every day little annoyances can make you feel angry.
When you can't just let it go,
When there is nothing to ruin your day even if it is being a MONDAY
How can you live and let live?
Well, life is full of things that will want to make you feel negative.
Smile at everything,
Soak it all in,
That is what life is about, feel that upset-ness
Learn why it made you feel upset and then just say bye!
If you must literally wave goodbye, then do so!
And then smile because it wasn't worth ruining your amazing day,
Just love and let love be

15

Do you surround yourself with people who love you
for you?
The happier you become
the more you see the right people surround you
The old ones fade away,
You'll meet and make more positive friends,
I know this from my own story,
I have people who love me as me
Surrounding us
giving each one of us the power to be better,
in a positive and supportive way.
It's the foundation of what we are as humans
It's all love no matter what.

15

Today I am grateful
For all, I do every single day is find gratitude
I am grateful for being able to walk
I am grateful to have electricity
I am grateful for water
I am grateful to do the dishes,
These are things I get to do,
This concept seems weird but it is amazing how quickly
It changes you and the way you look at life

17

Do you feel that when you hit a point of
Self-love, personal positivity, in all things.
Different happiness arrives altogether.
I wake up just happy, no matter what I have going on.
I smile, feeling love for everything.
It's the best feeling in the world.
You are never on a high
Or, then a low.
I feel genuinely happy.
When it all clicks,
I am just happy every day,
I woke up feeling something to reflect upon one
Morning,
DAMN AM I LATE FOR MY ARRIVAL.............
I am IN LOVE with WHO I AM
I am great.
You're not vain you just are!
It is the best feeling, you feel complete.
You are happy with yourself,
That is happiness with who you are

18

Yesterday can't be changed
So, look forward to today
Everyday is a gift
Smile that you are here one more day
So, show the world you
Spread your unique love to the world.

19

Self-reflection is an extremely important thing to do,
It's always a journey of reflection of one's self
With all truth and honesty, it is extremely humbling
I have faced so much in the time I am reflecting upon
And sometimes I am sad and think,
I messed up and take time to feel.
Sometimes it's minutes, sometimes hours or a day or two!
It is a part of growing and understanding yourself.
Knowing you are not better than anyone is key.
It is constantly learning.
You learn something new everyday.
Let that be at least one thing about you,
Learn and grow its joyful.
smile, you are amazing
This is you, your journey
It's YOUR story!

20

I am here
I am Present
It is all here for me to figure out
But I am not alone
I am loved
I am inspiring
I do more than I know
I am all I need
I will do this

21

Tiredness is what we accept as normal
But it is not,
Its our bodies saying something
Listen and you will hear it,
It means let it go
Recharge and make it better
A nap isn't a sign of weakness
It's a time to recharge YOU
Don't feel bad for it
Just do it.

22

Having the ability to make a change
Even a small change in someone else's life
Make that an Accomplishment.
Even if it was a smile, you did good
Inspiring and having impact on someone
Will be the best feeling
Moving you sometimes to tears
When you change
Others around will become happier as well
Their joy will make you happier
Happiness is the kind of pandemic I want
ITS EPIC
ITS JOY
It is mostly LOVE

23

Help others to be their best selves,
Encourage and support one another in all things
Remember that your Love is what they need
Live with empathy and kindness in your heart
Everyday give your gratitude for all you have
Be what you need to be in all you do,
Just be and love.
The day's drudgery isn't, that's a negative,
Look at it with a positive perspective ,
When you change the thinking on that
You change your way of things
looking at the simplest things with pleasure,
that will bring you simple happiness

24

When Negative people are constant
In your daily life,
Remember that they are not a reflection of you
These people can be your close loved ones
Wife, Husband, Children
Remember that it's a pain within themselves
They need love from you
But don't allow their negatives to be yours,
If they rub off on you
SHAKE IT OFF!!
Its not you, its them

25

Are there times where you feel so down?
Almost depressed down?
Make it known to yourself, it is ok
Knowing through consistent self reflection
We can handle these issues when they arise
I am confident that your daily doings will get better
You are strong and amazing
You will get through this!
There's nothing you haven't accomplished before
This is only one temporary situation
For within you is the power
To overcome this as you have before
Just breathe and it'll get better

26

Bitterness is not something to carry with you,
Its like Anger, its negative.
Love yourself for feeling this,
It might be just a lesson for you,
Everything you do is for you to learn.
There are signs everywhere,
You will know if you look,
The path is for you to take!
Watch and see the subtle signs
Its up to you to learn how to cope
Cope in the sense of learning you
You and what you need to do to let go
Move forward with a smile and love

27

Vision is about passion and love
Its more about what you really want,
It does take hard work and determination.
Nothing in life is free,
When you have a dream
Do what it takes to make it happen,
Feel that vibe, the happiness it brings you
But don't let anything stop you EVER!
Set out to fulfill them
And have the strongest faith it'll happen
Allow the universe to create it
Allow it to happen as it should,
It may take some time,
but determination that you have will never fail,
You will always succeed,
Not always the 1st, 2nd or even 12th time
But you learned more every time.
Live your dreams

28

When you finally decide to leave your negative behind
This may hurt you a lot but its necessary to do so
But remember that when you do
Its no one's fault, do not be mad
Their time in your life is done,
Cherish it and love it
Be grateful for what they taught you
Positive or negative
Go on being you
I see trees in the winter
I think what's more beautiful
The world is so beautiful
Ask your self one thing
Is it truly kind?
Or do you believe it is unkind?
It will hurt if you see it as unkind,
Everyday there is kindness
A bird sheltered in its home
Just like you
How is that not nice?

Don't think about the circle of life
Think of beauty in the bird,
Take in the moments
The views are amazing
Where there's kindness and beauty
From the beholder of the eyes and mind.

29

Good comes when you are good
Not the good as in you were good
But when you are happy, joyful
And all the problems you have
Are trees in the fore ground.
They seem like nothing even though they are there
Is there a great beauty within that?
Struggles, uncertainty, and fear
They are there, just a part of life
You don't run, you are thanks,
with pure Gratitude for it happening
give thanks to everything you have
tell your car, thank you
tell your bills, thank you
I am happy to have these things
Be glad for it,
Its strange but believe me it will change you
The stress goes away
You'll smile more, feel Good.
You will be sick less,

Feel life More,
Give yourself a pat on the shoulder
You made it this far
NOW KEEP GOING!!!

30

Creating the life, you dream of
Is the way to be.
I have desires, love and faith,
Its about Love.
This universe is kind and lovely
Love is the key everything we do
We are never to stop our faith
Imagine feel and receive
Imagine what you do want
Feel you have it
And receive it,
Give love and thanks to everything
Even if it seems silly and overboard
Be thankful and loving for all

31

Soul searching is a perfect start
On your road to where you will go
Know you are your own worst enemy
You are also your Best Friend
Be kind, but honest with you.
Make it known to you
Your Mistakes, accept them
Use it for your learning,
It will help you on your journey to happiness
In this world you will know you are better than anyone
Seek out the life you deserve
Know you are right where you need to be
This is your journey
But YOU are not alone

32

I found myself overwhelmed with all
I was crying at the simplest things with gratitude,
I was joyful and grateful
I feel happy and joyous
For today is MY DAY
I will succeed in everything I do

33

Why did you wake up this morning?
Why do you do what you do?
'Why' is a great thing to have!
Your why is what drives you
I have my why and it drives me
Accomplish what you want with your why
I love to cook
I love the colors
I love the flavors
I look at the uniqueness
The flavors that come out
When you add a little spice to it
I look at life like food
Its colorful
It beautiful
Its unique
Most of all it is flavorful
So, make the most of your colorful life.

34

The frequency you are on,
is it really the right one?
Energy is all around us,
Thoughts are how we control our lives
We become what we think,
STOP thinking about what you don't have
Stop thinking about what you don't want,
Start thinking about ALL you want,
We are surrounded by energy,
We are everything and can make everything we want
I know what I want,
I think about it,
I feel it to my core
I am not what I don't want
I am what I want.
I will create what I want.
I will receive what I want through love and giving.
I am my own positive force
No one will tell who I am
No one will tell who I am not either

I will define "ME" myself
I will prove I am worthy
Worthy of myself
Worthy of my love
I will discover my own worth
I will be patient
I will be kind
Best of all I will be loving to me.

35

Determination drives the imagination
Imagination drives your dreams
Dreams is where it starts.
So where do you get your determination
I look deep within and ask
Is this really what I want
Or will I forget this in a week
And move onto something else
I do that but that's because, I get bored
Or I get frustrated with it
So, I do another thing that is loving to me for the break
My life is filled with many passions and love
They keep me happy and smiling

36

I love children so much
They are so amazing and full of wonder
Wonder for the world
They have limited negative thoughts
Their experiences even if hurtful
They still love
They don't judge anyone
They just love,
The beauty of watching how children function
We should take a hint from them
Let's go back to our kindergarten principles
Remember the things we learned in kindergarten
Share, be kind to all, don't judge just love.
Let's get back to our human basics
Humility is our savior.
Humbleness is the remembrance of love
So, go be kids, and just live
Be simple and happy

37

Feel comfortable within yourself
All you do should be to make you healthy
The food you eat,
The water you drink
Give your body the nourishment it requires
For you will find it will help you
Not for energy,
For clarity of mind
For health of body
Relax for your tired
Its okay to be tired and exhausted
Its okay to take a break when you need
Its okay to make time for you
You are the only you
You are loved
And how can you be
Be as in the loved ones who surround you
And remain tired and exhausted
You will not be your best you
They will understand

And will love you anyways
WE ALL NEED A RECHARGE

38

My Love for the world
Its unshakable
Its underestimated
I love this world
In its beauty
I find peace within solace
Solace to love everything
Everything is beautiful
Life is wonderful and filled with love
Love solace and beauty everyday
All I do is find peace within all
Even anger, mistakes, and intensity
I will love this world the way it should be loved

39

Write yourself a letter
Make for 6 months from now
In 6 months open it
Where were you then
Where are you now?
Have you accomplished everything
Or even some of what you set out to do?
I did this and I was amazed at it
I looked back
I am so different now
I amazed myself,
I accomplished all of it then some
Make a year letter
Don't open it till that date
You'll be surprised when you look back
See yourself then
Look at you now.
I made myself.
I made things happen.
Love your journey

Fill it with joy and accomplishment
Be love and kind to yourself

40

I look to myself for inspiration
I realize that I am only me
I can and will inspire others
I inspire others by sharing me
I am REAL,
I am raw
My story will be inspiring
I will help others in their journeys
Because I was true to me
I was truthful.
I must continue to be me
For myself is all I have to offer
Take from me what you will
Make it positive and kind
I am only here to LOVE
I won't misguide you
I will only give the path to love

41

Do not get in your own way,
Create what you want
Its all within you
You are your own slave,
It starts within you
It will be your way,
We create our ailments
These things are created in us
When I am angry, I created that.
I choose to create joy, love, and happiness instead
I listen to me and deliver that truth
To live, to truly live
Is not to live without purpose,
Purpose is our drive,
Drive is where we get our determination from
Make it the way you want
Understand that you create the journey
If you understand what you feel is your choice
You are your own engineer
Create the You that you want,

Create the beauty that is within you
Create the manifestations that are you
Be happy with what you are
But always grow and study YOU

42

When I am overjoyed
I cry, I cry my heart out,
I feel over the top,
Nah, its not a high
To crash on and burn out
It's a high in happiness
And when I come down
I am still happy in all ways
Just keep smiling,
Keep being happy!
I love you because you are awesome

43

I found love in last place
I thought it would be
Where did you find love?
Who is he/she?
Nah, he/she was ME
I fell in love with me and who I am
I am awesome,
I am funny,
I am intimidating,
I will make you uncomfortable,
I am opinionated,
I love music,
I love to dance
I love to just be what the mood suits
As I am just me
I am awesome

44

Thank you for being in my life
I have gratitude for everyone in my life
I have never been so supported
I have never been so encouraged
Never have I felt such pride
In myself, but also for what I have accomplished
I can reflect how did I get here
Wow we are amazing people
I am thankful for what got to HERE
Goosebumps are Best friends right now
I have ARRIVED, late but I am here
How can I make you smile today?
Have a shower,
Put on your favorite outfit,
Do your Hair,
Do your make up
don't forget that lipstick you love
spritz your favourite perfume,
make this for you,
Dress up just because you can

You are all about you today
Look at you!
DAMN you look fantastic
Have a drink or 2 (wine is mine)
Dance in your Livingroom
Put that song on loud and repeat it
Just freak out for you
Feel your own vibe!

45

Be the best you can be,
You are all the world needs
You're the best for those around you
They love your vibe
They feel ya all the way
And never judge you for being you
They love ya no matter what
Cause you are good for their souls
You lift each other up
And never push each other down
My life took me in directions
Directions I never thought
Each corner had a surprise
Some good and some not so great
Some were extremely unexpected blessings
I have never been so thrilled
Filled with zest to succeed,
Visioning myself in all I'm doing
Feeling the truth as if it has happened
Living my life like its already mine

Living the truth.
The essence of one's true self is present
I am all I need to be and reached my point
The best self I can be.

46

Hurray! You are almost there
Its almost finished,
right at your fingertips
DO NOT STOP,
Keep the positive vibe going
Its more than positive
No, it wont mean there isn't failure
All this hard work wasn't for nothing
You are right there no matter what
Vision it, going well
Make it a true reality,
Like really believe it
I do this everyday
YOU GOT THIS ALL THE WAY!!
No love no stress
I ponder this with curiosity
No love, we need love
Does this mean love causes stress?
Nah, stress causes pain and suffering
Love brings happiness and joy

Have love have no stress
Don't worry be happy analogy
Blessed are we to the way we love
Don't forget to love you
And no stress for you

47

Never hide behind your mask
It'll never allow the world to see
You, and all that you are
Everyone needs to know
Just how spectacular you are
You sparkle in sun like rainbows after the rain
The skies upside down smile
When you look at the arch
It's the smile with color
Strikingly beautiful like yours
Feel good to know that after the storm
The sun shines and there's a rainbow
Smile back the beauty of that
They give us such beauty to see

48

Tranquility is something,
That we take for granted,
Meaning what to us?
Make yourself a tranquility spot
That's your place
Its your peace and quiet place
Make it a representation of you
And things that make you smile
It is meant to be your spot that you feel safe
Where you can calm
Where you are happy,
Forget the things that didn't make you at peace
Literally just empty your mind
This will become routine when
You are sad, angry, hurt, just negative
For me it is my kitchen with music

49

Personal health is key
To healthy mind
To healthy body
To healthy life
You don't need to be a health freak
To make exercise a routine
To make healthier choices in life
How can we build anything
Like self discipline
Like self determination
Become uncomfortable with the comfort
It'll Create self love and self pride

50

Dance is always a way to bring happiness
I have listened to many kinds of music
I learned about cultures this way
I learned about my respect for people
I took a major passion of mine
And expanded it
For me personally Afrobeats
Its my music which always brings happiness
At young age Africa was always beautiful.
It was my connection
It was the place that made me happy
Pick one and go for a trip.
The music, the life, the dance
They are my pieces of happiness.
Nigeria, Kenya, Tanzania, and South Africa
They always get me to my happy place

51

Make peace with your past
Who you were is not who you are,
Who you are will not determine who you will be
You are right where you need to be
The past created you NOW
Be happy and grateful for it
Celebrate it all
I do because I love who I am
What I am and who I will be

52

As the sun sets on another day
I am happy to have the sunset
On one more beautiful day
I have pushed myself so hard
I have made waves I shouldn't
But good has come from it
Always good,
I have made myself focus
I have Accomplished something
Was this a dream
I made that dream come true
I have struggled to make it happen
By mindset and vision
Created the visions to make this real

53

Thoughts are manifestations
We must really work towards
Our thoughts and our manifestations
Bring light to the darkness
Our love and passions are there
We ask we shall receive
I wish like the genie
Bring your vibe baby
You are needed to bring your light to the surface
Your everything IS NOW
Never look back with regret
Just take what you need not more
Use your senses, the 5 senses to bring what you want to you
Streetlight shine in the dark
As you walk by you see moths and bugs
They are attracted to the light
Think of you as that light
You are shining in the dark
Shining it for many to see

They will come to you
And you will all help each other to shine bright
And be beautiful

54

I must do this
I must do this
I will finish my goal
I am one step closer to my dream
The first step is done
The second step is done
The third one almost
The dream is almost a reality
I'm in love with this life
I am doing what I was destined to do
I am here to spread love
Be love and show faith

55

Be all you are
make your life shine
be free in your mind
there's nothing that will stop you
GO make reality of yours
Nobody changes you
You change yourself
You are exactly what you say you are
Are you your own hero?
YES, I am my hero
I am proud of me
I saved me from me
I saved me from my toxic relationship
The toxic one I had with me
I saved my damsel in distress
I scooped myself up in my arms and loved me
I got my happy ending
I got me, I got my back

56

My journey has always been going
It never ends as long as I live
I continuously study and learn
My road has been bumpy
Its also curvy and winding
I truly never thought I get to this point
But just to be here is all I need
I have come thus far
I will go even farther
Its to show me All I can do
This is my end, all be all
I will never escape death
So, live in my way
And manifest my dreams
GET Out there
Make your self known to the world
MAKE a name for yourself
But don't do it for greed
Don't do it for vanity
Surely never allow either to consume you along the way

Make your journey humbling
Make it honest
Accept truths that will hurt
Learn you are here for a reason
And find your reason
Live everyday for you
But not selfishly do something kind
Be loving to you but also others
Be Canadian, and say sorry a lot

57

Embrace the inner you
The one you are afraid to allow out
The right people will love you
The anxiety of those you make uncomfortable will disappear
You will learn to show you
All of you and the people around will love you
I thought I was too emotional
I was too boisterous
I learned that people love me for that
I for once was accepted to be
Happy lively and smiley
I'm greeted the same way I feel
I leave this with to remember
That we are all here together
Let's show that world functions on love
Not hate
We must remember we are human
Color makes nothing
Religion, sexual orientation

They exist in barriers that we create
So, love and be love
Spread love
Feed the hungry
We should never have to beg
We should be one
One human race of love
Today I revisited a part of myself,
From the past, I was feeling lost,
I heard music from that part of my life
I was feeling complete to me
I rediscovered that I need a bit of that person
I am who I was and will be
I loved then who I was
I also love who I have become.
I will find a way to reintroduce that part
It made me happy to feel it
But feel as the New me
I am the coolest person.

58

Love is life
Life is love
Be it
Feel it
Show it
Embrace it
We are love
And we live life
So, love is life
Life is love

ABOUT THE AUTHOR

Lindsay Woods is passionate about life. She loves to have fun and live life as should to its fullest. For Lindsay, writing is a way to vent the excitement and joy she feels for everyday life. There's always a smile on her face. Studying and a lover of education Lindsay finds herself in routine of reading and self betterment. Lindsay shares her experiences with a hope that through her writings someone will find solace in their everyday life.

Manufactured by Amazon.ca
Bolton, ON